DOPAMINE DETOX

A SHORT GUIDE TO ELIMINATE DISTRACTIONS AND TRAIN YOUR BRAIN TO DO HARD THINGS

THIBAUT MEURISSE

CONTENTS

WHO IS THIS BOOK FOR?

Do you keep procrastinating on important jobs? Do you often feel restless and unable to focus on the task at hand? Do you have trouble getting excited about the important goals that could improve your life?

If so, you might need a dopamine detox.

In today's world where distractions are everywhere, our ability to focus has become a scarce commodity. We're constantly being stimulated, feeling restless, often without knowing why. When the time comes to focus on the key tasks that would enable us to make progress toward our goals, we can often find a plethora of other things to do. Instead of working toward our goals, we might pop out for a walk, grab a coffee, check our emails or reorganize our files instead. Everything seems like a great idea—everything except the very thing we *should* be doing.

As we repeat this same pattern every day, we can let our biggest goals and loftier dreams slip between our fingers. We underperform and accomplish far less than we're capable of. And deep down we know it, which erodes our self-esteem and creates frustration, disappointment, apathy, jealousy, or even anger.

But it doesn't have to be this way.

When you learn to remove distractions and move away from this constant state of stimulation and restlessness, you can accomplish most of your challenging tasks. By doing so consistently, you will become more productive—and much happier as a result.

Are you ready to let go of unnecessary stimulations and reclaim your focus so that you can achieve your goals?

More specifically, in the 48h Dopamine Detox, you'll learn how to:

- Remove overstimulation and feel focused and peaceful during work,
- Feel naturally motivated to work on the key tasks that will enable you to reach your biggest goals (instead of procrastinating),
- Eliminate unproductive activities and distractions, and skyrocket your ability to focus, and much more.

If any of the above lessons interest you, read on.

INTRODUCTION

Tell me if this is you:

You know that if you could tackle just one specific task, it would have a massive impact on your overall levels of productivity. Perhaps it would improve your chances of earning a promotion. Or perhaps it would enhance your mental or physical well-being.

But you never seem to start.

Instead of working on your goal first thing in the morning, you end up checking your emails, looking at your stock portfolio, or scrolling your Facebook newsfeed instead.

Soon enough, that important task will appear less and less appealing. You tell yourself you'll just have one more coffee. Or you'll click on just one more YouTube video. But the more you delay your task, the harder it becomes to get started. It's as though an invisible mental barrier had appeared between you and your task, and this barrier seems impossible to overcome.

Have you ever felt this way?

If so, you'll greatly benefit from this book. In it, we'll introduce a simple method you can use to avoid overstimulation and make it easier to tackle your key tasks.

So, are you up for the challenge?

In **Part I. Dopamine and the Role it Plays**, we'll explain what dopamine actually is and how it works. After reading this section, you'll understand why you can't stop checking your phone, struggle to stay away from social media, or binge-watch videos.

In **Part II. The Problem**, we'll see why dopamine can be an issue these days. In this part, you'll discover how your dopamine transmitters have been hijacked and why this can be a major challenge.

In **Part III. The Benefits of a Detox**, we'll review all the reasons a dopamine detox can be useful. We'll introduce a number of different types of dopamine detoxes and we will discuss several misconceptions regarding dopamine.

In **Part IV. A Three-Step Method for a Successful Detox**, we'll explain in detail how you can implement an effective dopamine detox in three simple steps.

In **Part V. Doing the Work (and Overcoming Procrastination)**, we'll focus on getting you back to work. In this segment, you'll learn how to plan your day effectively and remove distractions to help you remain focused.

Finally, in **Part VI. Avoiding "Dopamine Relapse"**, we'll work through some simple tools and techniques to help you avoid overstimulation and stay focused on your key tasks over the long term.

Let's get started, shall we?

Your Free Step-By-Step Workbook

To help reclaim your focus I've created a workbook as a companion guide to this book. Make sure you download it at the following URL:

https://whatispersonaldevelopment.org/dopamine-detox

If you have any difficulties downloading the workbook contact me at:

thibaut.meurisse@gmail.com

and I will send it to you as soon as possible.

Alternatively, you can also use the workbook available at the end of this book

Boost your productivity now with The Productivity Series

This book is the first book in the **"Productivity Series"**. You can check out the second book, *Immediate Action* at the URL below:

mybook.to/immediate_action

PART I

DOPAMINE AND THE ROLE IT PLAYS

You've probably heard about dopamine before and have at least a vague idea of what it is. In this section, we'll briefly define dopamine and describe the role it plays.

Dopamine is a neurotransmitter which makes us anticipate rewards such as having sexual relationships or eating nourishing food. Dopamine gives us the desire to take action to earn the exciting reward that's waiting for us. It is the force that makes us act. As such, it is a very useful neurotransmitter that has helped us survive and reproduce—and probably one of the main reasons you and I exist today.

Contrary to what many people believe, dopamine is *not* a pleasure chemical. Simply because an event triggers the release of dopamine doesn't mean it is something we like or get pleasure from. In fact, when you pay close attention, you'll notice that as soon as you obtain the expected reward, you'll often feel empty and unfulfilled.

The truth is that no amount of stimulation will ever bring you the sense of fulfillment you're seeking. Yet, many of us are constantly overstimulated, looking for the next source that could trigger a release of dopamine. It seems as though we always want more and are never satisfied. And the more we seek stimulation, the worse it becomes.

Now, look at your own life. What are you addicted to? What do you crave? What are your main sources of stimulation? Do these things really make you happy?

As you consider these questions, you'll probably notice that you're addicted to highly stimulating activities (such as watching video games, immersing yourself in social media or reading emails). When you undertake these activities, you start losing self-control —you want more and more stimulation. And even though they may not give you any real pleasure or lasting fulfillment, you keep doing them. After all, you need the next hit of dopamine, don't you?

Under such a state of stimulation, any task that requires concentration becomes much harder to perform. As a result, you will procrastinate. You delay writing that book you've always planned. You put off starting that new venture, or you'll postpone that key project you're in charge of.

To sum up, from an evolutionary perspective, dopamine's role is to encourage you to act to earn the anticipated reward needed for your survival or reproduction. This is dopamine's primary role. Unfortunately, in today's world, the process has been hijacked, which leads to many unintended consequences, as we'll discuss in the next section.

* * *

Action step

Using your action guide, answer the following questions:

- What are you addicted to?
- What are your main sources of stimulation?
- Do they really make you happy?

PART II

THE PROBLEM

Previously, we've seen how dopamine plays an important role from an evolutionary standpoint. In this section, we'll see why this neurotransmitter has been hijacked and what you can do to guard yourself against the dopamine "traps" we face in today's society.

The neurotransmitter of more

You can think of dopamine as the "molecule of more". This is because the more our environment or actions trigger the release of dopamine, the more we'll want our next "shot" of dopamine. In fact, this self-reinforcing mechanism is also how many addictions work.

By continuously triggering the release of dopamine through different means—such as drug or alcohol consumption—addicts actually strengthen their tolerance to such stimulation. As a result, they need stronger and stronger stimulus to experience the same sensation of pleasure.

However, addictions are not just limited to drug or alcohol consumption. In truth, many activities can become somewhat addictive, for example:

- Gambling
- Sex
- Shopping
- Thoughts/rumination
- Video games
- Exercise (to extreme)
- Work

What about you? Are you currently addicted to anything? If you can't spend a day without engaging in a certain activity, it means you're probably a little addicted to it. Fortunately, as we'll see later, there are ways to limit the amount of stimulation we're exposed to each day. And, as we reduce our exposure to stimulating activities, we will naturally increase our focus and boost our productivity levels.

Now, let's see how your dopamine neurotransmitter is being hijacked in today's world. More importantly, let's see the specific things you can do to regain control.

* * *

Action step

Using your action guide, write down a past situation when you couldn't stop doing something. Are there any activities you can't stay away from for one whole day? Write it down as well.

Your dopamine neurotransmitters are being hijacked

Your focus is a scarce asset, which is why marketers spend billions of dollars to attract your attention. Many apps are designed to hook you. Social media companies like YouTube, Facebook, and Instagram know that the more time you spend on their platforms, the more money they make through advertising. Perhaps one of their greatest recent discoveries is the use of notifications. How many times have you opened an app just because a red notification pops up on your screen? And how much time did you waste subsequently? I wouldn't be surprised if it ran into hundreds of hours each year.

And, thanks to ever more sophisticated algorithms, companies have become better at hooking us. Amazon's book recommendation system is more accurate and widespread than any system a physical bookstore could create. Likewise, YouTube suggestions are heavily customized. And Facebook's customer research algorithm is quite amazing too. As a demonstration, try the following experiment:

Visit your newsfeed, watch a couple of suggested videos on a similar topic and see what happens. The other day I watched a basketball video and immediately received a recommendation to view another one, so I watched it. And then, I watched another one, and so on.

Now, the development of sophisticated algorithms has its pros and cons. On the plus side, it becomes easier to discover content you actually want to watch. On the negative side, it makes it easier to become stuck in a never-ending loop, watching one video after the other. In a sense, instead of using the internet to find information or communicate with loved ones, the internet has become the one using you. It does so by hijacking your focus and making you unproductive and, as a result, restless.

Social media notifications are a great example of how your brain is being hijacked. Whenever you see a notification, you anticipate the reward you'll receive when clicking on it, which triggers the release of dopamine in your brain. However, this doesn't make you happy or fulfill you—at least not for long. Remember, dopamine is not a pleasure chemical; it is a neurotransmitter that is activated when you anticipate a potential pleasure. And that pleasure is usually temporary. Below are some other ways your dopamine neurotransmitters are being hijacked:

- **Whenever you check your email**, you're expecting a reward, which could be a message from a friend or some exciting news.
- **Whenever you check stats**, such as investment portfolio, or website traffic stats, you expect a reward from seeing encouraging numbers. And the unpredictability makes it more exciting.
- **Whenever you visit YouTube**, you expect to watch interesting or exciting videos.
- **Whenever you visit social media sites**, such as Facebook, Twitter or Instagram, you're anticipating rewards such as likes or comments on your posts, messages from friends or interesting content.

When you engage in any of the above activities, you risk becoming not only overstimulated but also distracted and, as a result, you will lose your ability to focus. Whoever has succeeded in staying away from the internet or social media for a few days, understands what a waste of time and focus such activities can be.

What about you? How do you allow your dopamine neurotransmitters to be hijacked?

Food craving

Hunting for food used to be one of our biggest drivers for action. Hunger, alongside the anticipation of a great reward—food— leads us to act. And the food that gives us the most pleasure was highly nourishing, tasty, and often contained sugar.

According to Professor Susanne Klaus, a biologist at the German Institute of Human Nutrition in Potsdam, our craving for sweet foods is innate. Sugar triggers the release of dopamine and makes us feel good. She wrote, *"Experiments have shown that the combination of sugar and fat is especially effective in stimulating the brain's reward system."*

Therefore, it's hardly surprising that we like to get our daily dose of sugar and fat, is it?

However, these days, most of us live in a different environment. Although we still need to feed ourselves, the feeling of anticipation that drove our ancestors to search for food has become irrelevant. We can simply visit our local supermarket and buy what we want. There is no need to exert much effort. And, for most of us, food is plentiful. Yet, our biology has remained the same. We still experience that feeling of anticipation when being presented with rich food.

This is where the food industry comes in. In this industry, marketers spend millions to encourage us to buy their products. They discovered that, by adding sugar (among other things), they can not only make the food more palatable, but they make us crave more. For this reason, if you look at the list of ingredients contained in any processed food, you'll find sugar in most of them.

However, I should mention that, while there is a debate on the actual addictive power of sugar, it is unlikely to be as addictive as cocaine, as you might have read in some online articles.

Robert Lustig, professor of pediatrics at the University of California San Francisco, asserts that sugar is addictive but on the same level as nicotine, not drugs like heroin.

As Dr. Ziauddeen, a psychiatrist at the University of Cambridge, noted, *"The brain's reward system and the circuits that control eating behavior are the same ones that respond to drugs of abuse,"* but, unlike sugar, *"drugs of abuse seem to hijack those systems and turn off their normal controls."*

Furthermore, Tom Sanders, emeritus professor of nutrition and dietetics at King's College London, wrote, it is *"absurd to suggest that sugar is addictive like hard drugs."* He also said, *"While it is true that a liking for sweet things can be habit-forming, it is not addictive like opiates or cocaine. Individuals do not get withdrawal symptoms when they cut sugar intake."*

To conclude, humans seem to have a natural craving for sugar and fat. While we may not be addicted to them per se, it might be a good idea to reduce our intake and lower our dependence on them, especially on sugar.

Dopamine and constant stimulation can impair your ability to think long term

Studies have shown that one of the best predictors of success is the ability to think long term. People who repeatedly focus on where they want to be in the future, make better decisions in the present. They tend to eat healthier food, be more productive at work and save and invest more money than others.

After extensive research into success, Dr. Edward Banfield of Harvard University concluded that long-time perspective, *"was the most important determinant of financial and personal success in life."* He defined "long-time" as the *"ability to think several years into the future while making decisions in the present."*

Unfortunately, these days, focusing on our long-term goals isn't an easy feat. Many external forces lead us to become caught up in short-term thinking and encourage us to fall for immediate gratification.

While we often know what we should be doing, we fail to do it. For example:

- We know we should eat healthily but binge-eat on sweets or sugary beverages more than we should.
- We understand we should study, but we procrastinate by watching yet another series on Netflix.
- We can see the benefits of exercise, but we'd rather be sitting and chatting with friends on social media.

I believe that social media, and the internet as a whole, have negatively impacted our ability to both think long-term and to focus deeply on the task in front of us. It is no surprise, therefore, that Apple CEO, Steve Jobs, prohibited his children from using phones or tablets—even though his business was to sell millions of them to his customers!

The billionaire investor and former senior executive at Facebook, Chamath Palihapitiya, argues that we must rewire our brain to focus on the long term, which starts by removing social media apps from our phones. In his words, such apps, *"wire your brain for super-fast feedback."*

By receiving constant feedback, whether through likes, comments, or immediate replies to our messages, we condition ourselves to expect fast results with everything we do. And this feeling is certainly reinforced through ads for schemes to help us "get rich quick", and through cognitive biases (i.e., we only hear about the richest and most successful YouTubers, not about the ones who fail).

As we demand more and more stimulation, our focus is increasingly geared toward the short term and our vision of reality becomes distorted. This leads us to adopt inaccurate mental models such as:

- Success should come quickly and easily, or
- I don't need to work hard to lose weight or make money.

Ultimately, this erroneous concept distorts our vision of reality and our perception of time. We can feel jealous of people who seem to have achieved overnight success. We can even resent popular YouTubers. Even worse, we feel inadequate. It can lead us to think we are just not good enough, smart enough, or disciplined enough. Therefore, we feel the need to compensate by hustling harder. We have to hurry before we miss the opportunity. We have to find the secret that will help us become successful. And, in this frenetic race, we forget one of the most important values of all: patience.

No, watching motivational videos all day long won't help you reach your goals. But, performing daily consistent actions, sustained over a long period of time will. Staying calm and focusing on the one task in front of you every day will.

The point is, to achieve long-term goals in your personal or professional life, you must regain control of your attention and rewire your brain to focus on the long term. To do so, you should start by staying away from highly stimulating activities.

Here is a perfect illustration of long-term thinking:

Amazon, the world's third-largest company, was created in 1994 but had to wait until 2003 to have its first profitable year. That year, it generated a net profit of $35 million after reporting a net loss of $149 million the previous year.

Now, its founder, Jeff Bezos, could probably have made profits earlier, but, instead, he decided to reinvest in his business to create strong foundations that, he hoped, would enable Amazon to survive for decades. I encourage you to do the same in your personal and professional life. Build the foundations for success one brick at a time. Build them strong so that they won't collapse at the first obstacle or setback.

Remember, long-term thinking is the "secret" to achieving your goals. But it won't happen today or tomorrow. You must develop the art of patience and consistency. To do so, eliminate the distractions that make you feel restless. Remove the external stimulations that prevent you from focusing on the long-term picture. Then, you will stand a much better chance of ending up where you want to be in the coming years.

The bottom line is this:

In many aspects, today's society is designed to hijack your dopamine neurotransmitters. And, unfortunately, this is not designed in your best interest, it is designed to empty your wallet as effectively and thoroughly as possible. However, and more importantly, it dramatically erodes your ability to focus, making you feel restless and often bad about yourself. Overstimulated, you find yourself unable to do the difficult things that would have the greatest positive impact on your life and on the lives of people around you.

* * *

Action step

Using your action guide, complete the prompt below by being as specific as possible:

My brain is being hijacked when...

You're overstimulated

While there are many reasons to procrastinate, the most important one—and the one overlooked most often—is overstimulation.

When you are calm and focused, doing your main work can be surprisingly easy. You might even be excited, looking forward to making progress toward your biggest goals each day. However, the problem is that you're often anything but calm and focused. Instead, you're rushing through your day, jumping from one task to the next. You tend to run in circles like a hamster in a wheel, yet you never seem to complete your work. You let interruptions kill your focus and you waste hours checking your emails, visiting social media sites or watching one "educational" video after another.

It often starts first thing in the morning when you grab your phone. Then, it continues when you check your emails. But it doesn't stop there. You then decide to visit social media sites for "a few minutes". By that time, emails, notifications, and likes will have already triggered the release of dopamine into your system. In short, you've become overstimulated.

Now that you've received your dose of stimulation, you can work, right? But what happens when you sit at your desk to work on an important project? Does it come easy, or do you feel like doing everything else *but* working? Perhaps you tell yourself you can work on that particular task later. Perhaps you suddenly fancy another cup of coffee or perhaps you just remembered the email you need to answer.

Your work can wait—or so you think.

As a result, you're back into your hamster wheel, receiving more and more stimulation. This can last for hours or even days.

Do you recognize yourself in the above scenario?

The problem with overstimulation

When you're engaging in highly stimulating activities, your brain will keep demanding more and more stimulation. As your level of stimulation rises, regular tasks will appear increasingly dull and unappealing. You'll ask yourself, why work on my book, write a report or create a marketing plan when I could be doing something far more exciting?

The gap between your current high level of stimulation and the lower level of stimulation needed to tackle difficult tasks leads you to procrastinate. Picture it this way:

You're on a different stimulation wavelength, and this wavelength has no overlap with the wavelength you must be in to tackle your major tasks.

For instance, as a writer, my most important task is to write—obviously. However, as soon as I start checking social media, signing into YouTube or looking at my sales figures, I find myself pulled into a whirlpool of distractions from which I can't seem to escape. As my level of stimulation increases, writing becomes one of the most unappealing and challenging tasks imaginable.

Now, the key question is, what can we do about it? How can we lower our level of stimulation to make our major tasks appear more appealing and even exciting?

We're going to discuss this in the next section.

Action step

Using your action guide, write down a specific distraction pattern you often fall into that leads you to be in a state of overstimulation. For instance, it could be checking Facebook, then watching videos in your newsfeed before checking your emails and reading the news.

The stimulation traps

As soon as you enter a state of overstimulation, your mind will play tricks on you to convince you there is no need to leave that "trance". Instead, your mind encourages you to embrace it and seek even more stimulation. After all, we have to enjoy life, right?

In this section, let's go over four tricks your mind plays on you to keep you overstimulated.

Trick #1—returning to work is easy

The first trick your mind will play on you is to pretend that returning to work will be easy. It will try to convince you that you can start work whenever you choose, that you're in control of your actions. But this couldn't be further from the truth. In most cases, you won't be able to get back to work for hours. You might even find yourself postponing your key tasks until the next day.

The bottom line is, once you're overstimulated, you'll find it difficult to go back to work. I can't count how many times I told myself I would start writing later.

It never happens.

Therefore, if you catch yourself thinking you're in control of your actions and can return to work whenever you want, watch out!

Trick #2—you can do it later

Another trick your mind will use is to tell you that you can do your task later. It will convince you there is plenty of time in the afternoon or that you can always do it tomorrow, next week or next month. However, if you don't fight back, putting things off will become a habit. And five years from now, you'll be angry at yourself for having accomplished so few goals.

Trick #3—excitement is not the same thing as fulfillment

When you're engrossed in stimulating activities, your mind will sell you on how much fun and enjoyment you are having. You should do more of it. Don't worry about anything else for now. Just enjoy yourself. Or so your mind says.

But whatever your mind says, excitement doesn't equal fulfillment. Once your level of stimulation reverts back to normal, ask yourself the following questions:

How much did I actually benefit from watching YouTube videos, scrolling through my Facebook newsfeed, or checking my emails repeatedly? In hindsight, was the time spent in a meaningful way? Did it enhance the quality of your life?

Remember, excitement isn't fulfillment. Excitement can be fun, but make sure you work on developing an inner sense of peace and a heightened state of focus. This is much more likely to bring you fulfillment in the long run.

If you want to learn how to use your time both effectively and meaningfully in greater depth, read Book 8 in my *Mastery Series, Master Your Time*.

Trick #4—you're missing out

Checking emails or news every thirty minutes gives you the illusion of having some control over your environment. You don't want to miss an urgent email or the latest breaking news, right?

But do you always need to reply to emails right away? Do you really have to check the latest news regularly?

This way of thinking results from the fear of missing out. And this fear reflects a scarcity mindset, which is based on the idea that there might be a limited number of opportunities available to you. As such, you should seize each opportunity while you still can, shouldn't you? But opportunities are everywhere. There will always be more in the future. Thus, if you "miss" a piece of news, were unable to join a particular event, or failed to watch your favorite YouTuber's last live video, it's okay. Sure, I wouldn't recommend you miss the birth of your children or the wedding of your brother or sister, but for most events, it doesn't matter.

Personally, I seldom read the news and never answer my phone unless I know who the caller is. And I almost never worry about missing a specific event because I know there will always be more events to enjoy in the future.

What about you? Do you experience the fear of missing out?

As you go through your day, take note of whenever you fall into these traps. Awareness will help as you start to work on lowering your level of stimulation and becoming more focused on your goals.

* * *

Action step

Using your action guide, rate yourself for each of the following tricks on a scale from 1 to 10 (1 meaning you don't fall for that trap, 10 meaning it described your situation perfectly).

Trick #1—My mind convinces me going back to work is easy.

Trick #2—My mind tells me I can do it later.

Trick #3—My mind makes me believe that excitement is similar to fulfillment.

Trick #4—My mind tells me opportunities are limited.

PART III

THE BENEFITS OF A DETOX

The different types of dopamine detox and their respective benefits

So far, we've seen that one of the major problems preventing you doing the hard work is overstimulation. Therefore, the solution to tackling your major tasks is to reduce your level of stimulation. This is what the dopamine detox is for.

What is dopamine detox?

Dopamine detox describes the following process:

The reduction of stimulation to prevent overstimulation and put you in the proper state of mind to tackle major tasks.

Quick disclaimer:

Scientifically speaking, the term "dopamine detox" is incorrect as it seems to imply that you're releasing too much dopamine into your system. In truth, when you're overstimulated, you simply need more external stimuli *for the same amount* of dopamine to be released.

A dopamine detox helps reduce stimulation, thereby allowing you to revert to a more natural state. When you need less stimulation, seemingly challenging, boring or tedious tasks will become more appealing—and easier to tackle.

Now, let's have a look at the different types of dopamine detox available. In this book, I will introduce you to three distinct types as below:

- The 48-hour complete dopamine detox.
- The 24-hour dopamine detox.
- The partial dopamine detox.

Let's describe each process in greater depth and discuss how they work.

The 48-hour complete dopamine detox

This is the most demanding type of dopamine detox. The premise is simple:

You must eliminate most or all sources of external stimulation for a total of 48 hours. Doing so will help you reduce your overall level of stimulation and revert to your natural state. You will feel much calmer and find it easier to focus on any specific important task.

By "eliminating all external sources of stimulation", I mean you need to remove the following things from your life for 48 hours:

- Drug/alcohol consumption,
- Exercising,
- Internet,
- Movies,
- Music (except perhaps for relaxation music),
- Phone,
- Social media,
- Sugar/processed foods, and

- Video games.

Each of the above activities stimulates you, some more than others. Now, you might wonder:

If I eliminate these distractions, what should I be doing instead?

Here are some suggestions:

- Going for a contemplative walk,
- Journaling,
- Meditating/relaxing,
- Practicing awareness exercises,
- Reading (except stimulating read perhaps), and
- Stretching exercises.

As you can see, the 48-hour dopamine detox is intensive and might appear rather drastic. But it could be even more extreme. One of my friends, Nils, attended a Vipassana retreat, which is a 10-day meditation retreat. During the ten days, the participants are required to:

- Maintain complete silence (and have no gesture or eye contact with anyone),
- Have no physical contact,
- Take no physical exercise,
- Stop smoking, drinking, or taking any other drugs,
- Give up their phone and internet, and have no outside contacts,
- Avoid music, reading, and writing, and
- Avoid filming or taking pictures.

By comparison, the 48-hour dopamine detox sounds easy, right?

The 24-hour dopamine detox

This type is similar to the 48-hour dopamine detox but is, by definition, shorter. As such, although it will be easier, it will also be a little less effective. Note that it can take several days for your stimulation to revert to its natural level.

The partial dopamine detox

This type is less demanding, but it can be highly effective when maintained over a longer period of time. It entails removing your biggest source of stimulation. Usually, one specific activity acts as your greatest distraction. For instance, for me, it is YouTube.

What about you? What's your biggest source of stimulation?

In the next section, we'll see how to identify it and what to do to eliminate it effectively.

* * *

Action step

Using your action guide, write down which type of dopamine detox you want to implement right now.

PART IV

A THREE-STEP METHOD FOR A SUCCESSFUL DETOX

In this section, we'll go over a simple three-step method to help you perform a successful dopamine detox.

Step #1. Identify your biggest distractions

The first step to implementing an effective dopamine detox is to identify your biggest temptations and distractions. To do so, take a pen and a sheet of paper (or use your action guide), and create two columns, "Cans" and "Can'ts".

In the first column write down all the activities you will allow yourself to engage in. For instance, it might be going for a walk, journaling, working on a project, or reading books. In the second column, write down all the things you must avoid doing during your dopamine detox. For instance, it might be watching YouTube, checking your emails, or using social media.

To help you do this, ask yourself the following questions:

- If I stopped doing only one thing, which one would increase my focus and boost my productivity the most dramatically?
- What other activity do I need to avoid in order to help me increase my focus most significantly?

Keep asking yourself this question, until you're happy with your answers.

Once you have completed your list, put it on your desk or somewhere you will see it. It will act as a good reminder of the activities you must avoid.

Step #2. Add friction

Generally speaking, the harder something is to access, the less likely you are to do it and vice-versa. This is why you must redesign your environment to make undesirable behaviors more difficult to engage in while making more desirable behaviors easier to conduct.

Look at the habits or activities you want to eliminate and ask yourself how you could add friction—the more friction, the better. For instance:

- If your phone is your biggest distraction, remove all notifications or put it on airplane mode. Or, even better, switch it off and put it in a separate room.
- If Facebook is your biggest distraction, remove as many notifications as you can and/or use applications such as Newsfeed Eradicator (a Google Chrome extension).
- If you spend hours watching YouTube videos, install DF Tube on your Google Chrome navigator, or find a similar app for your internet browser. This will remove all the suggestions and notifications. Then, only watch videos that serve a specific purpose.

Adding friction might sound overly simple, but it works. This is because, as humans, we're fundamentally lazy. We hate wasting energy unless we are forced to. If you need to go to another room to grab your phone (friction #1) and also need to turn it on (friction #2), you are less likely to do it for a while. After I put my internet modem in my storage room, to get it back I needed to:

- Leave my apartment (friction #1),
- Take the elevator to descend four floors (friction #2),
- Open four doors (friction #3, #4, #5, and #6) to reach my modem, and
- Repeat the actions in reverse (friction #7 to #12).

This is a great deal of friction. Since I spent energy to take my modem to the storage room in the first place, my mind resisted getting it back right away. This would be a great waste of energy, which my mind doesn't like.

The bottom line is, the more difficult you make it to engage in unwanted behaviors, the better.

Conversely, make your desired behaviors as frictionless as possible. For instance, to facilitate writing in the morning, I avoid checking my phone or my emails and leave my word processor open. Then, I often put on relaxing music and use a timer (I like to do 45-minute work sessions). By doing so, I've removed friction and obtained the buy-in from my mind. It wouldn't make sense if I suddenly stopped the music, paused the timer, and moved on to another activity. My mind would see it as a waste of energy. Of course, I may still procrastinate, but removing friction and creating a simple routine reduces the chances of me doing so.

Your turn now. How could you add friction to eliminate unwanted behaviors?

- Look at your list of "Can'ts". Next to each of them, write down specific things you could do to *add* friction.
- Then, look at your list of "Cans" and write down things you could do to *eliminate* friction.

Remember, your mind is lazy. Use this to your advantage.

Step #3 Start first thing in the morning

The third and final step is simply to get started. I recommend you start first thing in the morning before becoming overly stimulated. I've noticed that if I check my phone or access the internet upon waking up, I will probably become distracted.

I also recommend you create a morning routine to help you start your day on a positive note and with a strong focus. Over the long term, a simple morning routine can make a massive difference in your life.

What about you? What's the first thing you do when you wake up? Does this help you remain calm and focused, or does it lead you to feel overstimulated and result in procrastination?

To establish your morning routine, write down two or three simple things you could do each morning. You'll use these activities to kickstart your dopamine detox—and, hopefully, you will stick to the routine over the long term. Remember that the routine should deepen your focus rather than stimulate you. For instance, you could:

- Meditate,
- Stretch,
- Listen to some relaxation music,
- Write down your goals for the day,
- Write down three things you're grateful for, or
- Repeat positive affirmations.

* * *

Action step

Using your action guide, create a simple daily routine to follow during your dopamine detox (and beyond).

To sum up, in order to implement a successful dopamine detox you should:

1. Identify your biggest temptations and/or distractions and write them down on the sheet of paper. Then, make sure you put the sheet in a prominent position.
2. Make unwanted behaviors harder to engage in by *adding* friction.
3. Make desired behaviors easier to engage in by *reducing* friction.
4. Implement a simple morning routine to calm your mind and start your day with a low level of stimulation.

Now, decide whether you want to do a 48-hour, a 24-hour or a partial detox. Then, identify the main sources of stimulation you'll eliminate as you go through your detox. For the 48-hour and 24-hour detox, try removing most, if not all, sources of stimulation. Stay away from the internet. Refrain from gambling. Avoid watching TV. Stop playing video games. Eat light meals free of sugar and processed food. Turn off your phone, and so on. For the partial detox, strive to remove your biggest source(s) of distraction.

Tips to make the most of your dopamine detox

Below are a few tips that will help you maximize the benefits you'll obtain from your dopamine detox.

Take notes

During your dopamine detox, I encourage you to take notes. If you feel restless, write it down. If you experience an urge to check your phone or to watch videos, write this down too. That way, you'll be able to identify your biggest sources of stimulation and learn more about the way your brain works.

Reflect on your life

When we're constantly busy and overstimulated, we sometimes fail to take a step back. We can't see the forest for the trees. Use your dopamine detox as a way to zoom out. To do so:

- **Reflect on your goals.** What goals are you pursuing? Are they the right ones for you? Are you making progress toward them each day? And if you keep doing what you're doing, will you reach them?
- **Assess how you're using your time.** Are you being truly productive each day? Do you spend time on things that matter? Which activities or projects do you really need to focus on? Which ones do you want to stop doing?
- **Self-reflect.** Are you where you want to be in life? What inner work could you do to improve yourself?

Solve your problems

If you have any problems or worries, write them down alongside potential solutions. Just putting your thoughts on paper can help you declutter your mind and gain clarity. This is because it's difficult to address thoughts that stay in your mind. You tend to ruminate on them. On the other hand, writing them down makes them more concrete. It helps clarify your thinking. By giving words to your thoughts (or worries), you can address them more easily.

I encourage you to take a pen and a sheet of paper and answer the questions above. In the absence of highly stimulating activities, you'll be calmer and more relaxed, and this, in turn, will allow you to develop greater insight.

More generally speaking, dedicating time to thinking each week can make a major difference in your life. It can prevent you making big mistakes and save you a great deal of time and energy. Therefore, refuse to let busyness be an excuse to avoid reflecting on your life.

Identify your fears

Finally, our never-ending search for stimulation is often an attempt to hide our fears. Being busy enables us to avoid having to face unpleasant feelings and scary truths about ourselves. Thus, if you notice certain disempowering thoughts or underlying fears, write them down too.

PART V

DOING THE WORK (AND OVERCOMING PROCRASTINATION)

One of the main goals of a dopamine detox is to lower your level of stimulation to help you feel more motivated to work on key tasks. In this section, we'll see what you can do to maintain the momentum and overcome your tendency to procrastinate.

Plan your day

Being intentional with your day is an effective way to boost your productivity. When you take time each day to decide what you want to accomplish, you limit the risk of distraction. Consequently, the more intentional you are, the better.

Planning your day is important for the following reasons:

- It gives you an opportunity to clarify which tasks are important and which ones aren't.
- It reduces the odds of your mind distracting you during the day. Because you know exactly what you have to do, you can move from one task to the next smoothly and without distractions.

- You will feel less stressed and more in control. Instead of reacting to your environment and letting it distract you, you will move toward your goals proactively.

How to plan your day

You don't need fancy tools to plan your day. Instead, you can use a secret technique forgotten by many—pen and paper. Simply write down a few key tasks you must achieve today. Three to five tasks might be ideal. Place them in order of importance and start working on your first task. Once you complete it, proceed to the next. Repeat the process until you have completed all the tasks on your list.

Now, here are a few things to consider:

Make sure these are key tasks that move the needle forward. To help you identify your major tasks, you can ask yourself the following question:

If I could complete only one task today, which one would have the greatest impact?

If you're still unsure, ask yourself this question:

If I could complete only one task today before taking a month off, what would that task be?

You'll notice that your most important tasks are often the ones you want to do the least. Perhaps, it's because they are challenging. Perhaps, you don't know where to start. Or, perhaps, they're boring. But your dopamine detox will help make these tasks easier to tackle.

Note that you can use the same method to set weekly, quarterly, monthly and yearly goals. I also recommend you create a long-term vision. It could be a five- or ten-year plan. Of course, it won't be perfect, but simply having an idea of the direction to follow will make a huge difference.

To set short-term goals, reverse-engineer what you must do to reach your long-term goals. For instance, if I want to write a book in the next ninety days, one goal could be to create an outline. Another could be to complete the first draft. And to hit that target, I could establish a specific daily word count.

* * *

Action step

Using your action guide or a separate sheet of paper, write down your daily and weekly goals.

Schedule one major task to work on each morning

While there are thousands of books on productivity, only a few principles matter. I believe the most important one is to identify your key task and tackle it first thing in the morning—and do this consistently.

Even though you might have a never-ending to-do list, there are always a few major tasks that, when completed, will skyrocket your productivity. Unless you can complete them, nothing else will really matter.

The key to productivity can be summarized in three words:

1. Focus,
2. Consistency, and
3. Impact.

1. **Focus** is your ability to maintain your concentration and avoid distraction or procrastination while working on your tasks.

2. Consistency means developing the habit of working on your key tasks every day, week after week, month after month, and year after year.

3. Impact means identifying your key tasks (the ones that have the greatest impact on your long-term success) and working on them as often as possible.

Productivity can then be defined as having **consistent focus on your most impactful tasks**.

Now, let's see what you can do specifically to stay focused on your most important task each day.

Develop laser-sharp focus

Your ability to develop laser-sharp focus is one of the most important things you can do to improve your productivity. By focusing on your key tasks consistently for just forty-five minutes daily, you can make more progress than you can with almost anything else you could be doing instead.

In this section, we'll discuss specific things you can do to build your focus and complete your key tasks each day.

1. Be at the same place, at the same time every day

As we mentioned before, a simple daily routine will help you condition your mind, help you feel more in control, and lower your stimulation. As a result, starting work will become easier.

One thing that will strengthen your routine is to be at the same place at the same time each day. The famous writer, Stephen King, sits at his desk every day at the same time and writes. He doesn't wait for inspiration to come. Instead, he starts, knowing that inspiration will come as he immerses himself in his work. Do the same thing. Choose a time and place where you'll be tackling your major tasks each day. Then, practice doing it one day at a time, and you will gradually build your consistency and focus.

Remember, productivity is nothing more than focusing on your most impactful tasks and doing so consistently.

What about you? Where will you be when you dedicate time to do your most important work, and when will you start?

2. Choose a trigger

As you create your routine, choose a specific trigger. It could be making tea and sitting at your desk. Or it could be completing your meditation session. Try to select a trigger that will help calm your mind. When you are relaxed, you'll find it easier to begin work.

What about you? What activity could kickstart your daily routine?

3. Get started

Once you have created your routine and identified your trigger, get started. If you can start work on your tasks for a few minutes, you'll likely build enough momentum to keep going. You might even experience flow. (Named by the psychologist Mihaly Csíkszentmihályi, the "flow" is a mental state in which you're so fully immersed in an activity that you become hyper-focused, while experiencing a sense of underlying enjoyment). Again, the more relaxed you are, the easier it will be to focus. So, just get started and don't worry about completing your task perfectly. It's okay if you don't feel motivated or creative, taking action *will* generate motivation and stimulate your creativity.

4. Eliminate distractions

When you work, remove all distractions. Turn off notifications on your phone, disconnect from social media and stay away from the internet unless it's needed for specific research. In addition, ask others not to disturb you. The more you practice working distraction-free, the stronger your focus will become.

5. Work without interruptions

Now that you have eliminated distractions, work continuously, without interruptions. I recommend forty-five minutes of intense work as a maximum. If you want to do several sessions, take a five-to ten-minute break between each work block.

Following the five steps above will strengthen your focus and boost your productivity. And, as you procrastinate less, you'll feel better, which will positively impact other areas of your life.

To learn more on how to develop laser-sharp focus, refer to book three in this series, *Powerful Focus*.

Action step

Using your action guide, follow the steps below to develop laser-sharp focus:

1. Decide what time you will focus on your key tasks. Then, make sure you're at the same place at the same time each day.
2. Choose a specific trigger to signal the start of your morning routine.
3. Just get started. When you work on your tasks for a few minutes, you'll be more likely to enter the flow and keep working longer.
4. Eliminate any distractions (phone notifications, internet, et cetera), and
5. Finally, work without interruption. Aim to complete forty-five minutes of uninterrupted work.

Beware of open systems

The activities with the biggest potential for distractions are usually part of an open system.

What is an open system?

An open system is simply an application or situation that provides you with a continuous and never-ending supply of external stimuli. Some examples are emails, Facebook, YouTube, and, more generally, the internet as a whole.

Whenever you enter an open system, you risk becoming overstimulated. For instance, if the first thing you do in the morning is to check Facebook, you might find yourself:

- Scrolling down your newsfeed for no reason,
- Watching one video after the next, or
- Messaging a friend and entering a long conversation.

Once you finally close Facebook, you might find yourself so stimulated, you'll struggle to begin work.

This is why you must guard against entering an open system—and understand the risk you take if you do so. With open systems, there is no end to reach, no point at which you can ever be finished, and an almost infinite number of ways to become distracted. As a result, you can end up wasting hours of your time each day. In short, open systems create distractions. Instead, you should strive to design closed systems.

What are closed systems?

These are systems that offer little or no room for distractions. As a result, they force you to work on your task—and only on it. Some examples are Excel spreadsheets, Word documents, or PowerPoint presentations.

These days, I strive to open the file for the book I'm currently writing, before doing anything else on my computer. I also avoid checking my phone. In other words, I start my day with a closed system, and I encourage you to do the same.

When you begin your working day with a closed system, you can avoid becoming overstimulated, which will make it easier for you to work on challenging tasks. And as you do so each day, you'll feel better and will want to work on even more tasks. So, perhaps one of the biggest secrets to overcoming procrastination and becoming more productive is to start your day with a closed system. This way, you can avoid countless distractions.

Remember, what you do first thing in the morning matters far more than you think. Just one tiny decision can have a dramatic effect on your day's productivity.

* * *

Action step

Using your action guide, write down a few examples of open systems that lead to you becoming distracted. Then, write down one closed system you could implement to help you increase your productivity.

PART VI

AVOIDING "DOPAMINE RELAPSE"

Congratulations! You've just completed a dopamine detox and now, I bet you feel much more relaxed and far more in control of your day. But what next?

If you're not careful, you'll inevitably relapse. Old habits die hard. That's why, in this section, we'll describe a few specific things you can do to avoid reverting back to your never-ending stimulation loop.

Let's get started.

1. Be aware when you start relapsing

Self-awareness is the key to making lasting change. The first step to avoid or limit relapses is to notice whenever you find yourself becoming overstimulated. When you struggle to work on an important task, stop for a moment. Then, recommit to your daily routine.

In truth, you will probably relapse after a few days, weeks or months. And this is completely normal. I find myself going from periods when I'm hyper-focused to periods when I feel restless and so overstimulated that I struggle to complete any work.

2. Understand the battle between you and your mind

When it happens to you, the key is to accept it and avoid feeling guilty. Beating yourself up won't help you build a successful daily routine. It will only make things worse. Therefore, don't dwell on it. Don't feel guilty or ashamed of yourself. Simply restart your routine and do it one day at a time.

3. Understand that the world is against you

In today's world, maintaining focus has become incredibly difficult. That's because everybody is vying for our attention. And I'm not just talking about our family members, friends, or colleagues. I'm also talking about marketers, YouTubers, or bloggers. Nowadays more than ever, the ability to attract people's attention is one of the biggest sources of income for many companies. In short, your focus is worth a lot of money, which is why YouTube, Facebook, and Instagram do everything they can to keep you glued to your screen.

However, your focus is also worth a lot of money to *you.*

When you reclaim your focus and use it to achieve your biggest goals, you can transform your life radically. You can make more money by channeling your focus into great work, and you can increase your well-being by redirecting it toward more meaningful activities (i.e., spending time with your family and friends or engaging in your favorite hobbies).

Here's my point. The world is working against you. There will always be someone trying to grab your attention. As such, you have two choices. You can protect your focus by building habits and systems, or you can remain unprepared and let anyone distract you from the important things you should be doing with your time.

Which option will you choose?

4. Prepare a contingency plan

An effective way to avoid relapsing is to create a contingency plan. To do so, think of all the ways you are likely to lose your focus and revert to your previous behaviors, and guard against them by creating a contingency plan.

So, what things could make you relapse?

For instance, if I check my phone first thing in the morning, I'll probably end up jumping from one stimulation to the next. I'll check Facebook, then perhaps reply to a message. This message may remind me of something else I need to do or it might give me ideas. Suddenly, my mind will become agitated and provide me with a plethora of good reasons not to write this morning.

To create your contingency plan:

- Consider all the activities with the highest potential for distraction. To identify them, revisit the list of "Can'ts" you created earlier.
- Envision the worst-case scenarios. What could lead you to lose focus and stop doing your morning routine? Using your action guide, write down all the worst-case scenarios you can think of.
- Prepare yourself mentally. Visualize yourself going through these scenarios. How will you react? Now, how would you *like* to react? See yourself dealing with these scenarios the best way possible.

5. Put a sustainable system in place

The key to lowering your levels of stimulation is to implement a simple and *sustainable* system. This system doesn't necessarily entail a complete shutdown from distractions, but it does require putting in place habits that will help you stay focused.

Consequently, as we've seen before, make sure you have a simple daily routine you can stick to consistently.

6. Cultivate the here-and-now neurotransmitters

To prevent overstimulation, cultivate the "here-and-now" neurotransmitters, which include endorphin, oxytocin, or serotonin. These neurotransmitters are the opposite of dopamine neurotransmitters in that they make you feel calmer and more present. To activate these neurotransmitters, incorporate activities that ground you in the present such as:

- **Meditation.** By meditating even for just a few minutes, you can practice being more "present in the moment". To do so, close your eyes and focus your attention on your breathing. You can also place your attention on one of your five senses. Then, switch to another sense, and another, and so on. There are no incorrect ways to meditate. Look for meditation books for beginners, search for meditation videos online, or simply experiment and see what works best for you.
- **Stretching.** When you stretch, you automatically relax your body and slow your breathing, which enables you to feel calmer and more present.
- **Mindfulness.** This means being aware of what's going inside you and around you. There are many ways to practice mindfulness. For example, you can eat slowly while noticing each flavor or texture. Or you can place your attention on your body and observe all the

sensations you're experiencing from head to toe. You could also practice completing household or work-related chores, while trying to be as present as possible.

- **Contemplative walking.** How present are you when you go for a walk? Do you hear the birds singing? Do you feel the wind blowing on your face? Do you notice the shape of clouds? Often, people become stuck in their head thinking of their next task or worrying about problems in their life. Don't be like them. Next time you go for a walk, observe things around you as if you were seeing them for the first time. Focus on each of your senses. See things you've never seen before. Hear sounds you've never heard before. Smell aromas you've never smelled before. Experience bodily sensations you've never noticed before. Be present!
- **Deep social interactions.** Interacting with other human beings activates neurotransmitters such as oxytocin, which is sometimes called the "love hormone". The more present you are, the more you'll be able to connect and experience a pleasant sense of bonding. Therefore, make sure you spend enough time around the people you care about.
- **Boredom.** Practicing doing nothing is a good way to lower your level of stimulation. Our mind constantly wants to do things. For a moment, be okay with doing nothing. Sit down and observe things, eat in silence or walk with no specific intent or destination in mind.

By incorporating some of the above activities, you'll be calmer and more present during your day. As a result, you will reduce the risk of becoming overstimulated.

What about you? What activities could you implement in your daily routine?

* * *

Action step

Using your action guide, write down at least one activity you could engage in every day in order to stay calm and focused.

Commit to a 30-Day Challenge.

To benefit from your dopamine detox, I encourage you to implement a simple daily routine to adhere to for the next thirty days. See it as a 30-Day Challenge. This will help you avoid reverting to your old habits as soon as you finish your dopamine detox.

Alternatively, you can read the other books in the series as you continue your journey toward higher levels of focus and productivity. Each subsequent book in the series will help you build a critical skill in just seven days.

• In **Book 2**, *Immediate Action*, you'll discover how to overcome procrastination.

• In **Book 3**, *Powerful Focus*, you'll learn how to gain clarity and develop laser-sharp focus.

• In **Book 4**, *Strategic Mindset*, you'll refine your critical thinking skills and develop a crystal-clear strategy that will help you skyrocket your productivity.

CONCLUSION

You can choose to control your focus, or you can let someone else take it away from you. When you learn to avoid highly stimulating activities that destroy your ability to remain calm and focused, you'll find yourself capable of tackling your major tasks with more ease than ever before. Going through a dopamine detox will help you lower your level of stimulation and ensure you work on your major tasks.

Remember that excitement and fulfillment aren't the same things. As you learn to eliminate external stimulations and immerse yourself in your work, hobbies, or relationships, you'll experience a deeper sense of fulfillment and will feel much better. You will also end up becoming far more productive and accomplishing many of your goals and dreams.

So, stop letting your environment hijack your brain and regain control of it instead. This is the key to a healthy and productive life.

OTHER BOOKS BY THE AUTHORS:

Crush Your Limits: Break Free from Limitations and Achieve Your True Potential

Goal Setting: The Ultimate Guide to Achieving Life-Changing Goals

Habits That Stick: The Ultimate Guide to Building Habits That Stick Once and For All

Master Your Beliefs: A Practical Guide to Stop Doubting Yourself and Build Unshakeable Confidence

Master Your Destiny: A Practical Guide to Rewrite Your Story and Become the Person You Want to Be

Master Your Emotions: A Practical Guide to Overcome Negativity and Better Manage Your Feelings

Master Your Focus: A Practical Guide to Stop Chasing the Next Thing and Focus on What Matters Until It's Done

Master Your Motivation: A Practical Guide to Unstick Yourself, Build Momentum and Sustain Long-Term Motivation

Master Your Success: Timeless Principles to Develop Inner Confidence and Create Authentic Success

Master Your Thinking: A Practical Guide to Align Yourself with Reality and Achieve Tangible Results in the Real World

Productivity Beast: An Unconventional Guide to Getting Things Done

The Greatness Manifesto: Overcome Your Fear and Go After What You Really Want

The One Goal: Master the Art of Goal Setting, Win Your Inner Battles, and Achieve Exceptional Results

The Passion Manifesto: Escape the Rat Race, Uncover Your Passion and Design a Career and Life You Love

The Thriving Introvert: Embrace the Gift of Introversion and Live the

Life You Were Meant to Live

The Ultimate Goal Setting Planner: Become an Unstoppable Goal Achiever in 90 Days or Less

Upgrade Yourself: Simple Strategies to Transform Your Mindset, Improve Your Habits and Change Your Life

Success is Inevitable: 17 Laws to Unlock Your Hidden Potential, Skyrocket Your Confidence and Get What You Want From Life

Wake Up Call: How To Take Control Of Your Morning And Transform Your Life

ABOUT THE AUTHOR

THIBAUT MEURISSE

Thibaut Meurisse is a personal development blogger, author, and founder of whatispersonaldevelopment.org.

Obsessed with self-improvement and fascinated by the power of the brain, his personal mission is to help people realize their full potential and reach higher levels of fulfillment and consciousness.

Learn more about Thibaut at:

amazon.com/author/thibautmeurisse
whatispersonaldevelopment.org
thibaut.meurisse@gmail.com

Follow him on Instagram at:

https://www.instagram.com/thibaut_meurisse/

ACTION GUIDE

Part 1—Dopamine and the role it plays

What are you addicted to? What are your main sources of stimulation and do they really make you happy?

Part 2—Dopamine, the problem

1. The neurotransmitter of more.

Write down a past situation when you couldn't stop doing something. Were there any activities you couldn't stay away from for one whole day? Write it down as well.

Activities you couldn't/can't stay away from for one whole day (if any):

2. Your dopamine neurotransmitters are being hijacked.

Complete the prompt below by being as specific as possible:

My brain is being hijacked when:

_____

3. You're overstimulated.

Write down a specific distraction pattern you often fall into and that leads you to be in a state of overstimulation. For instance, it could be checking Facebook, then watching videos on your newsfeed before checking your emails and reading the news.

Your distraction pattern:

4. Tricks your mind plays on you to keep you overstimulated.

Now, rate yourself for each of the following tricks on a scale from 1 to 10 (one meaning you don't fall for that trap, ten meaning it describes your situation perfectly).

Trick #1—My mind convinces me going back to work is easy

0   10

Trick #2—My mind tells me I can do it later

0   10

Trick #3—My mind makes me believe that excitement is similar to fulfillment

0   10

Trick #4—My mind tells me opportunities are limited

0   10

Part 3—Dopamine detox, the benefits

The different types of dopamine detox

Which type of Dopamine Detox do you want to implement right now?

Part 4—Dopamine detox, a three-step method to a successful detox

Now, create the simple daily routine you'll follow during your dopamine detox (and beyond).

1. Identify your biggest temptations and/or distractions and write them down on the sheet of paper. Then, make sure you put the sheet in a prominent position.
2. Make unwanted behaviors harder to engage in by adding friction.
3. Make desired behaviors easier to engage in by reducing friction.
4. Implement a simple morning routine to calm your mind and start your day with a low level of stimulation.

Write down your daily routine below:

Part 5 — Doing the work (and overcoming procrastination)

Write down your daily and weekly goals:

Daily Goals	Weekly Goals

Schedule one major task to work on each morning.

Identify your key task and tackle it first thing in the morning—and do this consistently.

Remember to follow the step below to develop laser-sharp focus:

1. Decide a time to focus on your key tasks. Then, make sure you're at the same place at the same time each day.
2. Choose a specific trigger to signal the start of your morning routine.
3. Just get started. When you work on your tasks for a few minutes, you'll be more likely to enter the flow and keep working longer.

4. Eliminate any distraction (phone notifications, internet etc.), and
5. Finally, work without interruption. Aim to complete forty-five minutes of uninterrupted work.

Beware of open systems

Write down a few examples of open systems that lead to you becoming distracted. Then, write down one close system you could implement to help you increase your productivity.

Open Systems:

_____

_____

_____

_____

_____

Close System:

_____

Part 6 — Avoiding "dopamine relapse"

Write down at least one activity you could engage in every day in order to stay calm and focused.

_____

_____

Commit to a thirty-day challenge.

To benefit from your dopamine detox, I encourage you to implement a simple daily routine to adhere to for the next thirty days. See it as a 30-day challenge. This will help you avoid reverting to your old habits as soon as you finish your dopamine detox.

Notes:

Notes:

60